5 HABITS
OF GODLY
RESILIENT
WOMEN

A Practical Guide and Workbook
for Making Strength a Lifestyle

AMANDA BEDZRAH

Copyright © 2017 by AMANDA BEDZRAH 2017

5 HABITS OF GODLY RESILIENT WOMEN
ISBN: 978-1-9999192-0-7

Published by:
The Vine Media Communications Ltd
Email: admin@thevinemedia.co.uk

Contents

Dedication

This book is for every woman who has, is, and will be going through challenges in life. God is with you every step of the way and He is using your challenges to equip you to do the good work that He has created you to do.

Genesis 50:20 NLT reads,
"You intended to harm me, but God intended it all for good. He brought me to this position so I could save the lives of many people."

You are part of a big picture and you won't be given more than you can bear. You have what it takes to hold on and scale through to the other side.

Acknowledgement & Thanks

To God's Holy Spirit – Thank you for the wisdom you give me to change my life and to share it with the world. There is nothing I can do without your guidance and direction. Thank you for directing me to write this manual. Your desire is to set women free, and I am humbled to be a vessel used for that purpose.

To My Husband Francois – Thank you for your love and continued support. Your constant encouragement keeps me going.

To My Children – Thank you for teaching me how to love and be patient. My life is so much richer because of the three of you.

To My Parents – You named me right. I am indeed a joy to the world. Thank you.

To My Sisters – You girls are my best friends. I love that you are always there.

To Joy Adeyemi – Thank you for giving me a reason to dig deep into this topic.

To My Friends – What can I say? You girls rock. I don't need to write down your names because you know who you are and how much I love you. I am truly blessed with great friends.

To Jennifer Rees Larcombe – Thank you so much for opening your door and heart to me. I have grown up in Beauty from Ashes.

To Papa John Bostock – You spoke words over my life that carries me day-by-day into the presence of God. You will forever be in my heart. Thank you for your father-heart towards me. It's an honour to call you dad.

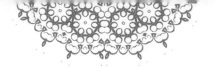

Foreword

By Jennifer Rees Larcombe

There are many things about this book that I really love! I always preferred books that are based on the Word of God - it gives me confidence, reassures me and gives me familiar words to hold on to. Amanda's book definitely does all that!

I like the way this book is broken down into sections – only a few of us have the luxury of reading a book in a sitting – most of us need "chunks" to chew on and take into the day with us.

Like many of us, I learn best when I have an opportunity to make notes or to journal; when I have read and studied truth, it is ingrained in me. This book asks such good questions for the reader to reflect on at the end of each sub-section, which makes you think deeply about what you need to have with record of lessons learnt and resolutions.

The language is very helpful and challenging, without making the reader feel uncomfortable, intimated or inadequate.

Above all, I like the fact that it is not just a "how-to" book, rather, Amanda's authentic voice shines through each page – her voice is that of a woman who has made the journey on this road herself, step by step.

I love her dedication to my dear friend 'Papa John' and the way she calls him her dad! This woman is so greatly loved by me and my family; she never ceases to amaze us.'

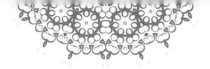

Introduction

I didn't set out to write a book on resilience. I didn't even think about that concept at the start! I wanted to simply prepare a short teaching to share with a group of women, but I have come to learn from my walk with God, that His ways are not ours. This scripture is very true in my life:

> *"'For my thoughts are not your thoughts,*
> *neither are your ways my ways,'*
> *declares the Lord"*
> *(Isaiah 55:8 NIV).*

I was asked to lead a *"Thrive Life Class"* by a dear friend, Joy Adeyemi, who runs a women's ministry called, *"We Are Thriving Women."* As part of the work they do, they run monthly Thrive Life Class sessions where various topics are discussed. I had the privilege of leading a class, and my topic was, *"5 Habits of Highly Resilient Women."*

In my own life, I have had to deal with a great deal of adversity, from childhood sexual abuse to severe depression. My life had been a rollercoaster, and as I look back at where God has brought me from, I can only see a woman who has stood firm in the face of adversity; a woman who

is still standing firm. By God's grace, I have learnt to make strength a lifestyle.

I made a commitment to God that by His grace, I would live my life with less of me and more of Him. As I prepared for the sessions, I prayed that God would teach me what He wanted His daughters to learn such that everything I shared would be what He wanted me to teach.

Yes, I know that I could effectively google five habits on resilience and share that using my own experiences as reference points to make it meaty, but there was a spirit of excellence that rose up in me encouraging me to do it God's way.

Every day I prayed and waited for God to show me His five habits. They didn't all come at once. Some came out of a song, a word I heard, or a scripture I read. Every habit I have shared in this book is a God-breathed revelation.

I am not sharing anything new with you. These habits are concepts that you have heard or read about before – what I believe will be new is the perspective and the context within which these habits are introduced and shared.

I invite you, dear woman of God, to open your heart and read this book with joyful expectation. There is something here that God wants you to read, a precious nugget that will change the course of your life forever.

What Is Resilience?

"You need to persevere so that when you have done the will of God, you will receive what he has promised."
Hebrews 10:36 NIV

I knew that I needed to define resilience in its true context as I started preparing to teach the topic. I had my own ideas of what resilience meant, but I still wanted to cross-check my thoughts with the dictionary definition. The word resilience according to the Oxford English Living dictionary means:

1. the capacity to recover quickly from difficulties; toughness
2. the ability of a substance or object to spring back into shape; elasticity

Both are great definitions and actually confirmed my thoughts; however, I wanted a definition that recognises the word with an element of empowerment to it. I wanted to personalise it and give it a definition that could be applied to our lives.

Therefore, I define resilience as:

"The strength to keep fighting and winning even when life's challenges become unbearable, knowing that in our weakness, God's strength is made perfect. [Therefore, we can stand firm in the face of adversity and not give up but instead give in to a God who saves as; we watch Him turn what was meant for evil into good for our good and for His glory]".

I love this definition because it instils a new confidence in me. It makes me feel like I can just let go and let God help me through the challenges in life. As Christians, we are not immune from problems—far from it. Jesus tells us in

John 16:33 NLT that,
"I have told you all this so that you may have peace in me.
Here on earth you will have many trials and sorrows.
But take heart,
because I have overcome the world."

It shouldn't surprise us when we face troubles in this world. The Bible clearly says that we would. Yet, as Christians, we forget and find it hard to believe that we can be saved but still experience trouble. We ask God questions like, "Why me, Lord?" Some people even think that a troubled life is an indication of continuous sin and a type of punishment.

The book of Job teaches us that the troubles Job encountered were not because he was a sinner but rather because He was a righteous son of God. His friends suggested it was because of His sin, but the truth is, he was being troubled because of his righteousness.

As Christian women, we will have challenges and we will have trouble, so we need to learn how to be resilient in the

face of adversity.

The first place to start, I believe, is found in

Ephesians 6: 10–18 NIV:
"10 Finally, be strong in the Lord and in his mighty power.
11 Put on the full armour of God, so that you can take your stand against the devil's schemes.
12 For our struggle is not against flesh and blood, but against the rulers, against the authorities, against the powers of this dark world and against the spiritual forces of evil in the heavenly realms.
13 Therefore, put on the full armour of God, so that when the day of evil comes,
you may be able to stand your ground, and after you have done everything, to stand.
14 Stand firm then, with the belt of truth buckled around your waist, with the breastplate of righteousness in place,
15 and with your feet fitted with the readiness that comes from the gospel of peace.
16 In addition to all this, take up the shield of faith, with which you can extinguish all the flaming arrows of the evil one.
17 Take the helmet of salvation and the sword of the Spirit, which is the word of God.
18 And pray in the Spirit on all occasions with all kinds

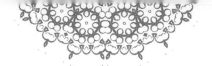

of prayers and requests. Be alert and always keep on praying for all the Lord's people."

Becoming resilient starts with understanding what we are wrestling against and preparing ourselves for the battle by putting on God's full armour to protect us so that we do not perish in the battles of life.

Decide to put on your full armour daily; leaving no place uncovered. The armour of God is not to prevent trouble but to protect you from experiencing painful circumstances.

In the next few chapters, it is my privilege to teach you the five habits that if applied, would make you more resilient. Firstly, let me ask you a question: Do you know your weaknesses?

This may seem like a silly question, but trust me, it is very important. We've grown up in a society that celebrates strength, a society that encourages us to focus on what we can do and worry less about the things we can't do.

During most job interviews, we are asked to talk about our strengths and weaknesses when actually, we are encouraged to talk about a weakness that can be perceived as a strength. I am not talking about one of those. I am talking about true weaknesses—think of and acknowledge the

things that you cannot do but are required to use to live life effectively.

Whilst there is wisdom in focusing on our strengths, we have an enemy that sets out to steal, kill, and destroy us. That enemy is the devil and he is a coward. He will kick a wounded horse when it's down and likes to capitalise on our weaknesses to make it easy for him to hurt us more effectively. We need to know our weaknesses.

One of my many weaknesses was my inability to navigate motherhood effectively, and I will share a bit more on that when we look at Habit 5. When the devil wanted to bring havoc into my life, that caused me to plunge into deep depression, he came through my role as a mother. I was so focused on doing the things that I could do and left unguarded, the things I could not do. Consequently, the devil slowly but surely, came into my life and caused me adversity like never before.

I praise God for his deliverance and that He always makes His strength perfect in our weaknesses. God has taught me that when we walk in our strength, we are involved; when we walk in our weakness, He is involved. It is very important that you take time out to acknowledge the areas in your life where you need God's strength.

I encourage you to pause and do the exercises at the end

of this and every chapter as they will help you on your journey to becoming a resilient woman of God. Don't overlook this step and jump right in to the next chapter. Take the time to work through these questions, and to pray.

I am privileged to share God's truths with you, but it is my desire that you get a personal revelation from each chapter for yourself. Ask God to teach you personally what He wants you to learn, and make notes that you can refer to over and over again. Don't just read this book; make it your personal journal for a personal journey. Work through it, and watch God work through you.

Let's Pray

Dear Father,
thank you very much for being with me in every area of my
life. I ask that you open my heart to receive your truth. I
pray that your Holy Spirit will fill me with understanding
and bring comfort and peace into my life.
I pray that even as I go through the difficulties in life, you
will give me the grace and strength to carry on. I ask that
you fill me with godly resilience, and I thank you for all that
you are doing in my life.

In Jesus' name, Amen.

Write your own prayers

....

....

....

....

Workbook 1

Reflect on Resilience

Q1 How will YOU personally define RESILIENCE?

....

....

....

....

....

....

Q2 What has struck you most about this chapter?

....

....

....

....

....

....

Q3 Write down all 7 PARTS OF GOD'S ARMOUR, and think about ways you can apply them daily.

1. ....

2. ....

3. ....

4. ....

5. ....

6. ....

7. ....

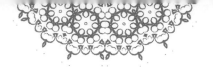

Ways to apply them

....
....
....
....
....
....

Q4 What are your WEAKNESSES?

....
....
....
....
....
....

Q5 In what areas of your life do you require Resilience?

....
....
....
....
....
....

Find and write out scriptures that will encourage you on this habit

....

....

....

....

....

....

....

....

....

....

....

....

....

....

....

....

....

....

Notes

....

....

....

....

....

....

....

....

....

....

....

....

....

....

....

....

....

....

....

What Is a Habit?

"Something That You Do Often And Regularly, Sometimes Without Knowing That You Are Doing It"
-English Dictionary

HABIT 1
Give Thanks for Adversity

"But Giving Thanks Is A Sacrifice That
Truly Honors Me. If You Keep To My Path,
I Will Reveal To You The Salvation Of
God."
Psalm 50:23 NLT

HABIT 1

I t is not easy to be thankful when life gets hard. To be honest, the last thing you want to do is be thankful, yet the Bible instructs us to give thanks in every circumstance. Why can't we just wallow in self-pity and grieve over our circumstances? How can we be thankful for adversity?

I must admit, when God gave me Habit 1, I initially struggled with it. I reflected on all my past situations as well as my present ones, and I really didn't feel thankful.

I have a lot of memories of the day my brother died over 20 years ago. Although I was very young, I would never forget my mum running into the house screaming, with tears,

"THE BIBLE SAYS WE SHOULD GIVE THANKS," over and over again. It confused me at first; I thought a miracle had happened, but later I found out my brother was dead, and I could not understand why my mum was giving thanks anyway.

As I grew older and started reading the Bible, I found the scripture in

1 Thessalonians 5:18 NKJV that says,
"In everything give thanks; for this is the will of God in Christ Jesus for you,"

Even though I could accept it as scripture and now understand why my mum behaved the way she did, I still found it hard to grasp the meaning and importance of giving thanks in adversity.

My light bulb moment came one evening as I sat observing a teaching on resilience in 2015. A YouTube video was played of Joni Eareckson Tada as she talked about her life, from being an active young girl with dreams, preparing to go to university, to then having a swimming accident that left her quadriplegic and the impact that made in her life. Joni also talked about 1 Thessalonians 5:18 and the discomfort she felt when someone who visited her in the hospital told her to give thanks. She then went on to say that the lady that was speaking to her reminded her that the scripture instructs us to GIVE THANKS not FEEL THANKS.

This was such a revelation to me that I could feel sore in my heart about my circumstances but still walk in obedience by saying, *"Thank you, Jesus."* I suddenly understood what my mother did many years ago.

There's a huge difference between what we feel and how

we should react. God needs us to give thanks despite how we feel because the truth is, the circumstances will change, and we will look back on our troubles and realise that God worked it out for our good. Our ability to give thanks is a declaration of trust. It is us saying, *"God, here's my situation…I know you are in control."*
It's not an easy thing to do; that is why it is a habit we need to learn.

I don't know about you, but personally, I have been through some situations that make me want to crawl under my covers and just stay there. I don't want to talk to anyone; I don't want to smile, and I don't want to do anything to change the circumstances, because I don't even want to try. I.JUST.WANT.TO.BE.

Have you ever felt that way? I'm sure you have. Then we come across scriptures like

James 1:2–4 NIV that says,
"Consider it pure joy, my brothers and sisters, whenever you face trials of many kinds, because you know that the testing of your faith produces perseverance. Let perseverance finish its work so that you may be mature and complete, not lacking anything,"

Such passages make you wonder whether you've missed a trick. Well, the truth is, yes, you have missed a trick because, the things that ought to break us are the very

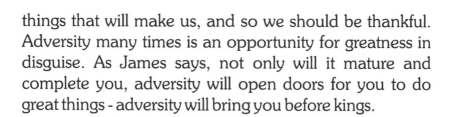

things that will make us, and so we should be thankful. Adversity many times is an opportunity for greatness in disguise. As James says, not only will it mature and complete you, adversity will open doors for you to do great things - adversity will bring you before kings.

We need to learn how to say thank you to God for our troubles because they are stepping stones to take us higher in life. King David grew up in the middle of adversity. He was the youngest and by default, got the job of being the shepherd boy; looking after farm animals, but it was in this place of difficulty that he learnt the skills that helped him fight his giant.

In the wilderness, he had killed a bear and a lion, he knew who his God was, and he had learnt to lean on Him and trust in Him regardless of His circumstances. King David needed Goliath. Yes, he did, killing Goliath gave him a position of influence and an experience that he needed and would not have had otherwise.

Joseph needed his brothers to sell him into slavery as that set the scene for everything else to fall into place. There are many other accounts in the Bible that teach us that we can grow through and in adversity, and our ability to stand firm and give thanks to God even in the midst of it will help us overcome things, which will work for our good and for God's glory.

Giving thanks in adversity is about taking the focus off our problems and putting the focus on God. It is not about erasing what we feel—challenges are tough and painful to deal with—it is about choosing to walk in obedience to God's Word and understanding that your adversity is not about you—it is about what God wants to do through you. It is about the lives that God wants to change and the person God wants you to become.

God knows that it is not easy to give thanks during a storm, and that is why Psalm 50:23 calls it a SACRIFICE, yet also a blessing. Psalm 50:23 teaches us that we honour God when we give Him thanks even in situations we don't understand and for things we can't control or change. We do it in obedience to His Word and claim the promises that it brings.

Therefore, the first habit we must learn is to approach our challenges with a new perspective. Instead of complaining about the difficulties in life, be thankful for them. Instead of wishing your problems away and praying for God to take away the struggle, saying, *"Why is this happening to me?"* ask God, *"What do you want to do through me? Where do you want to take me? What influence do you want to give me?"* And then ask Him to show you the internal resource that you can use to overcome your adversity.

The truth is, we have all we need within us. Think about

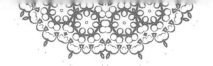

David—he defeated Goliath with a slingshot and a stone. He used the resources he already had; he didn't need the king's armour or a sword—he used what was in his hand instead, which was magnified by the God who was in his heart. He came to Goliath in the name of the Lord.

By God's grace, you have everything you need to succeed. Give thanks now. Don't wait till you feel thankful. Walk in obedience and give thanks, and you will be filled with the strength, courage, and multiplication that comes out of a spirit of thanksgiving.

Remember, this is a habit that we need to cultivate and make a part of our lifestyle. In all things, we should choose to give God thanks. It may not be something you are used to doing, and maybe this is the first time you have heard this, but it is never too late to start. Simply make the commitment to try, and day by day, you will find that it would become easier to give thanks. You don't need to give thanks only in adversity; give thanks all the time, and watch it become a habit that will change your life for good.

I encourage you to pause and take the time to do the exercises at the end of this chapter as they will help you on your journey to becoming a resilient woman of God. Don't overlook this step and jump right in to the next chapter. Take the time to work through these questions, and take time out to pray.

I am privileged to share God's truths with you, but it is my desire that you get a personal revelation from each chapter for yourself. Ask God to teach you personally what he wants you to learn from each chapter, and make notes that you can refer to over and over again. Don't just read this book; make it your personal journal for a personal journey. Work through it, and watch God work through you.

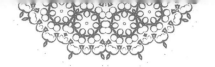

Let's Pray

Dear Father,
I admit that giving thanks in the middle of the troubles of life
can be difficult when my heart is hurting, and I am filled
with fear and confusion, when my trust has been broken
and my mind is disillusioned, when I don't know what to do
or who to turn to. Lord God, it is hard to find the strength to
say thank you, but your Word commands that in all situa-
tions, we should give thanks.

Teach me how to give thanks even when I don't feel thank-
ful, teach me how to take my eyes off my troubles and fix
them on you, and show me your heart for me in every
situation.
In Jesus' name. Amen.

Write your own prayers

. . . .

. . . .

. . . .

. . . .

Workbook 2

Reflections on Habit 1

Give Thanks for Adversity

Q1 Write out and meditate on Psalm 50:23.

....

....

....

....

....

....

Q2 What struck you the most in this chapter?

....

....

....

....

....

....

Q3 What adversities have you overcome by God's grace?

....

....

....

....

....

....

Q4 What current situations do you need to give God thanks for?

....

....

....

....

....

....

Q5 What are the skills and abilities that you have that God can use to change your situation?

....

....

....

....

....

....

Find and write out scriptures that will encourage you on this habit

....

....

....

....

....

....

....

....

....

....

....

....

....

....

....

....

....

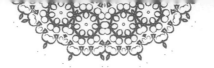

Notes

....
....
....
....
....
....
....
....
....
....
....
....
....
....
....
....
....
....
....

HABIT 2

Live in the PRESENT with and in the PRESENCE of God

"But as for me, how good it is to be near God! I have made the Sovereign LORD my shelter, and I will tell everyone about the wonderful things you do."
Psalm 73:28 NLT

HABIT 2

I didn't remember my childhood of sexual abuse until the year I turned 28. Even though my brain blocked out the painful memories from my childhood, somewhere inside of me, I knew something was wrong with me—I just didn't know what it was. When the memories came back, it came with more heartache than anyone should bear. Sometimes, it was easier to act like it didn't happen and force myself to forget it than to deal with the truth of the memories.

I used to think my life was a movie and I got to play a part. I would watch myself do such horrible things that came out of feelings of rejection and self-hatred, yet I was unable to change my behaviour, and I didn't understand why. All I knew was that I was unlovable and nobody truly loved me; I had to do everything I could to buy or earn people's affection. Somewhere in my mind, I had formed the belief that I didn't deserve to be loved and that I was a terrible person.

This meant that I was a very fearful and anxious person. Although I felt alone in this world, I had some internal companions that I could rely on. They were shame, guilt,

fear, anxiety, worry, anger…the list was truly endless, but those were my best buds. Even when I started a new relationship with God and was released from the bondage of the religion I grew up with, I still struggled to deal with the issues I had in life.

I could not understand why—why didn't I have the strength to fight? What was it that I was doing wrong? Why was I so weak? Even when I prayed, tried and wanted to be strong, I ended up with a mess of it all.

Being a wife and a mother with three children had its own challenges. My life was filled with things that I could worry about, things that left me in a fit of anxiety and many times in deep depression. I was also dealing with the shame and regret that came out of my youth and the effects I suffered because of my abuse.

What I didn't know was that I lived my life like a rocking chair, moving back in regret and moving forward with anxiety. And that is exactly how the devil wanted me to live—in the past and in the future but never in the present. Why? Because we serve a God who exists in the present and who wants to walk and journey with us through our lives in the now. The devil knows this and doesn't like that, so instead, he keeps us swinging back and forth like a pendulum that never stops to enjoy moments with God. A place where we can find the strength to go on.

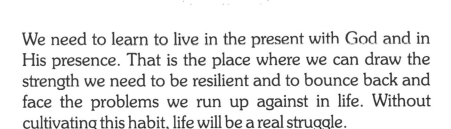

We need to learn to live in the present with God and in His presence. That is the place where we can draw the strength we need to be resilient and to bounce back and face the problems we run up against in life. Without cultivating this habit, life will be a real struggle.

I love the Bible account in Exodus when Moses was being sent to the Israelites and he asked God, "Who should I say sent me?"

Exodus 3:14 NIV says,
"God said to Moses, 'I AM WHO I AM.'
This is what you are to say to the Israelites:
"I AM has sent me to you"."

I never got a full revelation of that scripture until God started to speak to me about living in the present. That scripture suddenly came alive to me because I realised that God is I AM, not I WAS or I WILL BE. God is I AM. He is, now.

It made no sense for me to have suffered with regret, shame, and guilt from my past and lived in such anxiety about my future, because I was simply walking in my own strength, and it was leaving me exhausted, tired, and overwhelmed. There was no resilience in me at all. I couldn't cope with life.

To bring change into my life and have the strength I needed to fight each day, I had to understand this simple

truth and apply it to my life daily:

🦋 LIVE IN THE PRESENT WITH GOD AND IN THE PRESENCE OF GOD.

God was in my past, God will be in my future, but he is here now, and that is exactly where we need to be with God—HERE NOW. He is our ever-present help in times of trouble. There is nothing that we are going through that God doesn't go through with us. He is there in the middle of our pain and brokenness, and we need to decide to live in the present with God.

The Bible tells us in

Isaiah 43:18–19 NIV,
"Forget the former things; do not dwell on the past. See, I am doing a new thing! Now it springs up; do you not perceive it? I am making a way in the desert and streams in the wasteland."

The truth is, we can't do anything about the past; it has already happened. Neither can we control the future. All we can do is declare, like King David did in

Psalm 118:24 ESV,
"This is the day that the Lord has made; let us rejoice and be glad in it."

Let us rejoice in this day, in this moment, with our God,
who is I AM.

To live in the present with God is not easy if we try to do it in our own strength. It takes time and discipline, but the right foundation is a willing heart—a heart that yearns to seek God every day and enjoys God in the present and in His presence.

Our ability to live in God's presence is heavily reliant on our ability to trust him. Think about the Israelites in Exodus 16, where we read of God's daily provision. His instruction to them in verse 4 was to gather a day's portion. The ones who didn't obey and gathered too much were left with rotten food the next day. That came out of fear and lack of trust; fear that asks, "Will He be there tomorrow?"

God's grace, His provision, and loving presence are new EVERY MORNING. All we have to do is make a conscious decision to walk daily with God.

Lamentations 3:22–23 ESV says,
"The steadfast love of the Lord never ceases, his mercies never come to an end; they are new every morning; great is your faithfulness."

Find freedom and strength in this truth: God's love never ceases; His mercies are new every morning. Relax, girl,

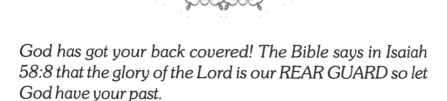

God has got your back covered! The Bible says in Isaiah 58:8 that the glory of the Lord is our REAR GUARD so let God have your past.

Jeremiah 29:11 NIV reminds us,
"For I know the plans I have for you," declares the Lord, "plans to prosper you and not to harm you, plans to give you hope and a future."

Therefore, let God hold your future.

"So, do not worry, saying, 'What shall we eat?' or 'What shall we drink?' or 'What shall we wear?' For the pagans run after all these things, and your heavenly Father knows that you need them. But seek first his kingdom and his righteousness, and all these things will be given to you as well. Therefore do not worry about tomorrow, for tomorrow will worry about itself. Each day has enough trouble of its own."
- Matthew 6:31–34 NIV

Remember, that this is a habit that we need to cultivate. We need to take the time to practice living in the present with God and in His presence. It will take time to learn to focus daily on God, so be patient with yourself and hold on to this truth: God's grace is new EVERY MORNING; we cannot carry it over or save it for the next day. It gives us the strength to fight today, and if we don't focus on it or welcome it, we will miss it. Don't miss it.

The devil wants to distract you and prevent you from enjoying every day with God because he is very jealous of God's love for us. The Bible is filled with the truth of the love of God for us.

Zephaniah 3:17 NLT says,
"For the LORD your God is living among you. He is a mighty saviour. He will take delight in you with gladness. With his love, he will calm all your fears. He will rejoice over you with joyful songs."

I love this scripture. I love the image of God singing and dancing because of His love for me—a love that saves, rejoices, and calms me. That is the love of God that we can enjoy every day with him and in him. Don't let the devil use fear, worry, and anxiety to rob you of that love. Here are some practical steps that will guide you:

♪ HOW TO LIVE IN THE PRESENT WITH GOD

Speak to God always – He is interested in everything that concerns you. Yes, He knows your worries and concerns, but you acknowledge your need for Him to share them and be a part of them when you choose to share them with Him. God truly wants to be with you.

Focus on today – Leave yesterday alone, and don't worry about tomorrow. Find scriptures that remind you that God has your past and future, and say them often. Be

active in reminding yourself that your life is in God's hands, and regardless of what you are going through now, He is a good God and will work it out for your good.

Be honest with God – Tell him everything as it is—not what you want Him to hear, or what you think is holy enough to be said, but the truth. Don't hide your thoughts or emotions from God. Don't think He only wants to hear the "big things". Everything that concerns you is important to God. God loves honesty, and His Word says that He delights in it.

Proverbs 12:22 tells us,
"The Lord detests lying lips, but he delights in people who are trustworthy."

🕊 HOW TO LIVE IN THE PRESENCE OF GOD

Get to know God – Spend time with Him, Talk to Him, and read the Bible (His Word). He loves to have your attention. Make this your priority, and fit your life around your time with God; don't fit God around your life. Seek Him first always, and then you will get everything else added to you (Matthew 6:33).

Remember that God is a holy God, and when you become a woman of God, you carry God's Holy Spirit within you. Be mindful of how you talk, act, and think.

Don't defile yourself intentionally and still think you can come freely into His presence. He is a holy God. You don't have to be perfect, but you must choose not to dwell in sin or take His grace for granted.

Hebrews 12:14 NIV says,
"Make every effort to live in peace with everyone and to be holy; without holiness, no one will see the Lord."

Most importantly, ask God to show you how to live in His presence. If your desire is to seek God, then He won't hide from you. He will let you find him. He wants to be in fellowship with you. We were born and created for that purpose, therefore, to not be in the present with God and in the presence of God is to deny yourself your very purpose of existence. Your life will feel meaningless and empty, yet there is only one person who can fill the gap. Turn to Him. He is waiting.

I encourage you to pause and take the time to do the exercises at the end of this chapter as they will help you on your journey to becoming a resilient woman of God. Don't overlook this step and jump right in to the next chapter. Take the time to work through these questions, and to pray.

I am privileged to share God's truths with you, but it is my desire that you get a personal revelation from each chap-

ter for yourself. Ask God to teach you personally what He wants you to learn from each chapter, and make notes that you can refer to over and over again. Don't just read this book; make it your personal journal for a personal journey. Work through it, and watch God work through you.

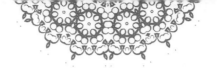

Let's Pray

Dear Father,
I know you love me so much that you want to be involved in every area of my life. You want to talk to me and walk with me. Teach me, Lord, to live in the present with you that I may be aware of you and draw the strength I need from you each day. Teach me, Lord, to be in your presence always; to find comfort in your constant protection.

Show me your father's heart towards me that I may experience a love, so true and deep. Help me to realise that my deep hunger and thirst is for you, and please fill me with your living waters.
In Jesus' name. Amen.

Write your own prayers

....

....

....

....

Workbook 3

Reflections on Habit 2

Live in the PRESENT with and in the PRESENCE of God

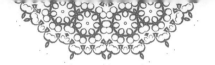

Q1 What has struck you most about this chapter?

....

....

....

....

....

....

Q2 Read and meditate on Psalm 91, and write down your thoughts.

....

....

....

....

....

....

Q3 How do you think you can develop a more intimate relationship with God?

....

....

....

....

Q4 What will it mean for you to live in the present with God?

....

....

....

....

....

....

Q5 What scriptures can you find about God's presence?

....

....

....

....

....

....

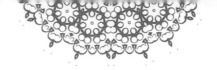

Find and write out scriptures that will encourage you on this habit

....
....
....
....
....
....
....
....
....
....
....
....
....
....
....
....
....
....

Notes

....

....

....

....

....

....

....

....

....

....

....

....

....

....

....

....

....

HABIT 3
Choose to FORGIVE
and LET GO

"Then said he unto the disciples, It is impossible but that offences will come: but woe unto him, through whom they come!"
Luke 17:1 - KJV

HABIT 3

Can I be honest? Of all the habits God has taught me, this is the one that has challenged me the most—the habit of forgiveness! It feels like the moment I was given this habit to teach, I was suddenly presented with so many ways to practice it before I could effectively teach it myself. I had to take a break from writing this guide for a while to deal with the issue of unforgiveness in my life.

In life, you will get offended. Yes, you will. As sure as there is day and night, there will be offence. There will be big offences, small offences, and some life-changing ones. Therefore, it is wise to expect it. There is freedom in being able to embrace this truth, so I will say it again: YOU WILL GET OFFENDED!

When the Holy Spirit spoke to me about forgiveness being a habit for resilience, I didn't immediately see the connection nor understand why. My first thought was how are these two connected? I know that it is important to forgive—certainly it is something that God has commanded us to do—but what I didn't initially understand was the relationship between forgiveness and resilience.

And so, God showed me.

I had been doing lots of reading and praying and learning on forgiveness, and I prayed a dangerous prayer: "God, give me a forgiving heart." I bet you are wondering why I refer to that as a dangerous prayer. Well, the way God works is when you ask him for something, He will give it to you, but the only way you will know for sure that you have it is by exercising it. Suddenly, the flood gates of offence opened, and now I had to exercise my forgiving heart.

It wasn't easy, and it still is not easy today. A lot of stuff from my past came up again—issues I had not properly dealt with or handed over to God, things I had held in my heart towards others, and, more surprisingly, things I had held in my heart towards myself. Do you know it has been so much easier to forgive other people than it has been for me to truly forgive myself? This revelation was a huge shock to me.

What I have learnt that I must now share is that it takes a lot of energy to be offended. It takes a lot of mental energy to hold onto an offence, to process it over and over in your mind and to feel that anger and rage within you.
If you are holding on to an offence, then you are not going to have the strength to move ahead in life. Un-forgiveness is like a poison that filters through the mind and fills you with anger and bitterness. It will prevent you

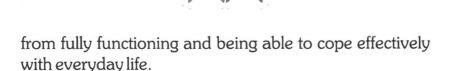

from fully functioning and being able to cope effectively with everyday life.

It is a subtle destroyer and it's not an apparent evil, which is what makes it very dangerous. You can't easily connect the cause with the effects, therefore, when things start going wrong in your life in unexpected ways, you won't see that the root of the problem is 'un-forgiveness'. Besides, the devil likes an unforgiving heart and will use it to his advantage.

Therefore, we are warned in

2 Corinthians 2:10–11 (NLT) –
"When you forgive this man, I forgive him, too. And when I forgive whatever needs to be forgiven, I do so with Christ's authority for your benefit, so that Satan will not outsmart us. For we are familiar with his evil schemes."

Be very aware of the devil's scheme. Know that the command to forgive is for our own protection as well. Such is the love of the Father that He teaches us to let go for the sake of the things that can bring more pain and chaos into our lives.

Let me give you two examples of offence from my own life and the effects it has had. I always say that I am not afraid to be vulnerable if it will inspire or perhaps em-

power another woman to do better, so I will try to be as transparent as possible.

Being offended by others – The people that have challenged me the most are my three children. Motherhood is not something that has come naturally to me, and in Habit 5, I will share a bit more about that, but for this example, I will be honest and say that sometimes my children really upset me. I believe I do a lot for them, yet, I get very little from them in return. They can be selfish and this has brought me to tears many times. There are times that I think such unholy thoughts about them, and I get very angry about the foolishness in some of their actions, consequently, I have held on to certain things that they have done.

The effect of that, however, shows in the way I behave towards them. When I am already bitter and angry and holding on to a memory of what they have done, the next thing they do in addition to that leaves me screaming at them, smacking them, or running into that bathroom to cry my eyes out. Why? Because I have unforgiveness in my heart that leaves me unable to deal rationally with a present situation.

I had NO RESILIENCE, and so I crumbled. No strength to fight. No strength to do what is right. Sometimes, it could be unforgiveness from things done in the past which they have forgotten but I still remember.

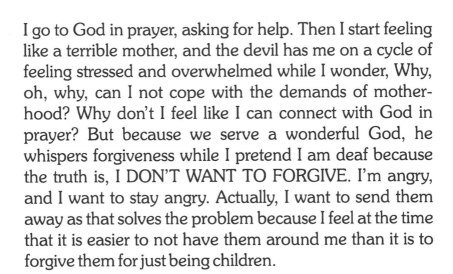

I go to God in prayer, asking for help. Then I start feeling like a terrible mother, and the devil has me on a cycle of feeling stressed and overwhelmed while I wonder, Why, oh, why, can I not cope with the demands of motherhood? Why don't I feel like I can connect with God in prayer? But because we serve a wonderful God, he whispers forgiveness while I pretend I am deaf because the truth is, I DON'T WANT TO FORGIVE. I'm angry, and I want to stay angry. Actually, I want to send them away as that solves the problem because I feel at the time that it is easier to not have them around me than it is to forgive them for just being children.

Doesn't that sound irrational? Doesn't that sound a little crazy? Doesn't that sound even more wicked that whatever silly thing it is the children have done? It does. Each time I step back and revisit my actions and thoughts, I see clearly that my 'un-forgiveness' does not just damage them—it damages me! How could I not see that? Why was I opening the door for the enemy to come in and rob me of the joy and happiness life has to offer because I choose to hold on to bitterness instead?

It damages me in ways that reflect on both the inside and the outside. It influences the way my children are brought up and behave towards each other and their peers, because the truth is, kids don't listen—they copy. And so, I have kids who behave in the same way I behave when they are offended.

I am very grateful that God has taken time to show me this and to teach me better ways to manage my heart by making an instant decision to forgive when offence comes. Immediately I say, *"Lord, help me forgive. I choose to forgive. I am going to let go,"* and I extend grace to them.

I love my children, all three of them. They truly are the kindest and sweetest. Their behaviour is because children are who they are—children—yet many times, it is I who behaves like the child with the way I act and respond. Parenting is hard work. It requires you to be selfless, and I have learnt this the hard way while learning how important being able to forgive is in raising children. I draw my strength for parenthood from my ability, by God's grace, to wipe the slate clean and start over each day.

Being offended with myself – I never really understood the importance of forgiving myself. It is so much easier to acknowledge offence against others than it is to realise that you are angry with yourself. Yet this is such an important thing to do because unforgiveness towards yourself breeds self-hatred, and when you hate yourself, you damage yourself from the inside without even knowing it.

For many years, I have tried to control my weight. I grew up as a skinny child—so skinny that I was teased consistently in high school. I even became bulimic in my older teenage years as I tried to force myself to gain weight but then felt guilty afterwards and would force myself to throw up. It just became a nightmare of a cycle.

As a young adult, birth control pills and then motherhood enabled me to gain the weight I so desperately wanted, but then the constant adversities in life taught me to comfort eat so that I eventually became overweight. It doesn't help that I am allergic to all painkillers, so when I am sick physically or emotionally, I would eat myself silly to feel better. Then I would hate myself for it…and so another cycle emerged.

I have yo-yo dieted, taken all manner of pills, and have spent hundreds and thousands of pounds on temporary fixes but still ended up going back to square one, and yet I could never understand why. I'd pray for inner healing and get professional help, spiritual help, and deliverance on many occasions, but it all came to nothing. NOTHING!

However, something happened one day. I can't remember what I was doing or where I was; it wasn't anything spiritual or important, but I remember the prompt, the whisper, the question: "Why are you so angry with yourself?" Have you ever had a thought that literally takes your breath away and leaves you speechless or mentally immobile?

Over a period of months, God showed me that I had not truly forgiven myself. Yes, the effects of being sexually

abused had left me bitter and broken, and so I made very poor choices and did things I regret, I'm ashamed of, and wish that I didn't do. Those things were slowly eating me on the inside and I didn't even know it.

My inability to truly forgive myself for what I had done in response to what was done to me meant that I was treating myself very badly and was punishing my body by eating much more than it needed. I was deliberately opening myself to sickness, stress, and poor well-being simply because I had not forgiven myself. My moods, my attitudes, and my emotions were all being tied into my negative perception and behaviours towards myself. My life was suffering and falling apart so subtly within my own control and by my own hands because of my unforgiveness towards myself.

I am not saying here that everyone who is overweight is overweight because of self-hate—not at all. There are lots of genetic and health reasons that can be the underlying factor for being overweight. However, in my own life, being overweight was a direct reflection of my inability to truly love myself by treating myself with the love and respect I needed. That could only have happened if I placed value on my body, instead of giving in to gluttony.

As soon as I realised that I truly needed to forgive myself and go on an inner healing journey with Jesus, I thought all was okay and I would begin to see immediate changes like some people testify. Honestly, I thought that would happen, but I have come to learn that God is a miracle worker, not a magician, and He chooses as He pleases. However, this is real life, not a fairy tale; God mostly expects us to lead the change.

God healed my heart and walked with me on this ongoing journey to truly forgive myself and let go, but I needed to work on my character and change my bad eating habits. I still needed to learn how to run to God for comfort and not food. I had to make the right choices, but I didn't have to do it in my own strength. I now had God's help too.

You see, habits can be good or bad. They are very difficult to form and even more difficult to change or get rid of. It is still an ongoing journey. It is not easy, and I am not yet where I want to be, but praise God, I am nowhere near where I used to be! I am on a journey of self-discovery and self-love, and I am learning not to internalise my mistakes but to forgive myself for my past and present thoughts, words, and actions as frequently and as often as I need to. I have also learnt to be quick to ask for forgiveness from others and to acknowledge my own wrong actions and responses to situations. These days, I find myself asking my kids to forgive me.

There is something humbling about giving and receiving forgiveness. Personally, it reminds me of the cross. God

did not ask us to forgive just so that other people can get away with doing wrong things to us. No, God, in His all-knowing love for us and with our best interests in His heart, understands that unforgiveness damages us much more than we could ever imagine. It imprisons us and leaves us bitter, angry, and unable to fight the good fight that we are called to.

I must say that unforgiveness is not about forgetting what happened, but instead, it is about remembering what God has done for us and what He will do with us and through us—even through those things that are painful. It is about learning to trust God in all things and knowing that He is a good God and He will fight our battles for us.

There is the temptation to want to do it our way and to punish those who hurt us in our own strength and with our own devices. Many times, the weapon we use for that is unforgiveness. It is as though we think that because we remain angry with the person, it makes a difference in their lives; it really doesn't.

Do you know that most times the people who offend us forget the offence? Even the ones who remember what they did don't care enough to let your unforgiveness bother them.

They sleep comfortably at night while you are awake, angry and frustrated and are thinking up ways of hurting them, plotting the ultimate revenge, or waiting for something bad to happen to them so that you can gloat and be happy that they got hurt. However, if you step back and think about the thoughts and emotions that I've just described, you will see that if you hold this perception, you are just as unloving as the person who hurt you.

I am in no way excusing their bad behaviour, neither am I taking for granted, the hurt and heartbreak that come out of terrible situations. I have been there, and I know what it feels like to wish someone dead—many times I even wished that someone was me—but I have learnt to view forgiveness through the same eyes that I view giving thanks in adversity—I forgive based on my obedience and not my feelings.

It's not my job to control my emotions nor is it necessary for me to mend it—that's for Jesus to do. It is my job, however, to choose, of my own free will, to walk in forgiveness, and to forgive as God commands. The Bible never said that we need to feel forgiveness; it says that we need to forgive. This is so close to God's heart that it forms part of the Lord's Prayer. It is so close to God's heart that many parts of the Bible show that your forgiveness from God hinges on your ability to forgive others.

We need to learn to detach what we feel from what we do. As women of God, we must learn the habit of forgiveness in response to obedience and not emotions. We are, by

our nature, feelers. We feel things, and can act out of our feelings, but that is very dangerous; we need to learn how to act out of the Word of God.

We are all in need of forgiveness, and all make mistakes; we all fall short. We cannot expect to receive what we are not willing to give—the Bible makes that clear.

Matthew 6:14–15 is clear on this: Forgive others so you, too, will be forgiven; if you don't forgive, then you also will not be forgiven.

Think about it…what is important to you? Is it more important to have God's mercy than it is to hold on to an offence? The answer to that should be what guides and informs you.

Peter asked Jesus in Matthew 18:21–22 how many times we should forgive, and His response was interesting, He said 70 times seven, which, if calculated, is about 20 times every hour. Jesus knew we would get offended, and Jesus also knew we needed to forgive as frequently as we get offended.

Luke 17:4 NLT also makes it clear by saying,
"Even if that person wrongs you seven times a day and each time turns again and asks forgiveness, you must forgive."

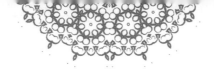

God is a God of justice and vengeance; in His own time and in His own way, the terrible things that have happened to us, and the things that have offended us will be judged and dealt with.

Jesus said in Luke 17:1 NIV,
"Then Jesus said to his disciples, "things that cause people to stumble are bound to come, but woe to anyone through whom they come"

There is something about that word "woe" that fills me with confidence that Jesus will sort it out, so that I can forgive and let go.

🕊 FORGIVENESS TIP

Remember, forgiveness is not about what you feel; it's about walking in obedience to God's Word. Your willingness to forgive will not erase the hurt from the offence nor will it wipe out the memory.

However, when you do feel the pain or when you remember what happened and anger wells up within you, decide to pray. Yes, pray! Let your remembrance of the offence be your reminder to pray. Just say *"Lord, I choose to forgive, and I ask that you heal these emotions."* It's an easy prayer, but it is very effective. The devil likes to remind you about past hurts and wants to use them to torment you.

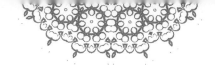

However, when your response to those emotions is prayer, trust me; he will not be in a hurry to remind you again. There is nothing he hates more than a praying woman.

I encourage you to pause and take the time to do the exercises at the end of this chapter as they will help you on your journey to becoming a resilient woman of God. Don't overlook this step and jump right in to the next chapter. Take the time to work through these questions, and take the time to pray.

I am privileged to share God's truths with you, but it is my desire that you get a personal revelation from each chapter yourself. Ask God to teach you personally, what He wants you to learn from each chapter, and make notes that you can refer to over and over again. Don't just read this book; make it your personal journal for a personal journey. Work through it, and watch God work through you.

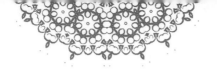

Let's Pray

Dear Father,
thank you that your love for me is so vast and deep that
even while I was still a sinner, you sent your only son to
come and die for me. You forgive my own sins, and you
extend unlimited grace to me not out of duty, but from an
undying love. Father, I bring all my hurt and pain to you. I
lay down all my offences at your feet and ask for your grace
to let go; to leave them at the cross and walk away. I pray,
sweet Jesus, that you will heal the hurt that remains and
bless me with a love that is much stronger than hate.
Bless me, Father, with a forgiving heart, and teach me how
to walk in obedience to your Word despite my emotions so
that I would be a woman who walks out of the truth of your
Word.
In Jesus' name, Amen.

Write your own prayers

....

....

....

Reflections on Habit 3

Choose to FORGIVE
and LET GO

Q1 What has struck you most about this chapter?

....

....

....

....

....

....

Q2 Read Matthew 18:21–35, and write down your thoughts.

....

....

....

....

....

....

Q3 What other scriptures can you find about forgiveness?

....

....

....

....

....

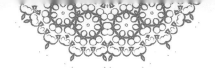

Q2 What steps can you take to make forgiveness a habit?

....

....

....

....

....

....

Q3 Who do you need to forgive? Pause and pray, asking God to show you, and then write their name(s) down. Release them to God.

....

....

....

....

....

....

Find and write out scriptures that will encourage you on this habit

....

....

....

....

....

....

....

....

....

....

....

....

....

....

....

....

....

....

....

....

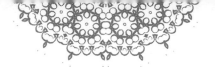

Notes

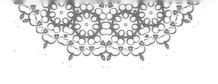

HABIT 4
Strength through REST in God

"And I gave them my Sabbath days of rest as a sign between them and me. It was to remind them that I am the LORD, who had set them apart to be holy."
Ezekiel 20:12

HABIT 4

When God started speaking to me about rest, I initially thought it was in the context of simple rest. It made sense to me because I was tired, in every sense of the word—physically, emotionally, and spiritually. I was constantly wiped out. I have struggled with depression for many years, and one of the main episode triggers for me is tiredness and stress.

As soon as I am stressed and tired, I start to get overwhelmed, and if I don't put in measures to step back, then I end up in depression without the will or ability to cope with everyday life. This can go on for days, weeks, or even months depending on the season or situation.

As I continued to speak to God to find ways to cope, ways of being resilient and not letting life overwhelm me, the word REST kept coming up. I assumed I was not resting enough, and so sometimes I would go away to rest. I would stay in bed all day. I would shut down, hide away, or do all I knew how to do to rest.

But it made no long-lasting difference; very quickly, I would find myself back to square one, questioning God—why wasn't I feeling better? Why wasn't I re-

freshed? I still struggled with being stressed and over-whelmed, and I didn't really know what I needed to do to change the situation, beyond what I was already doing. I was getting fed up with it all.

A few months ago, I was preparing some teaching notes about deception and how it started at the fall, and I had to refer to the beginning of creation in Genesis. I have read Genesis many times, but for the first time,

Genesis 2:2 NIV, suddenly struck me. It says,
"By the seventh day God had finished the work he had been doing; so on the seventh day he rested from all his work,".

It was at that point that I realised that God was speaking to me about the SABBATH REST.

It wasn't that I had forgotten about the Sabbath rest or that I didn't even know it was a commandment, but somehow, I just never really grasped that it was some-thing that I personally needed to do.

To be honest, a part of me thought it was a Jewish thing, another part thought it was an Old Testament thing, and I think the last bit of me thought it only applied to certain Christians that attend a denomination that observe the Sabbath day. I just never thought about it at all. The minute God highlighted it to me, it was all I could think

about. I just could not shake this longing for observing this rest. I became desperate to understand it and its significance more, and so I started asking questions, researching, reading, and praying. Luckily, I know a friend who is a Seventh Day Adventist, and I could get some useful information from her, but more importantly, I turned to the Word and started to look for scriptures to get some understanding of the Sabbath rest.

WHAT IS THE SABBATH REST?

The word Sabbath is from the Hebrew word SHABÀT, meaning "cessation" or "time of rest". The Bible tells us in Genesis that God worked for six days and rested on the seventh day from all His labour. He just stopped and chilled. The Sabbath rest is basically taking one day off from all your work and spending it with God and your family.

When I started doing some research into the Sabbath, I was excited about it, but it seemed like a big luxury, something that I couldn't afford to do. I remember having a conversation with God as I tried to explain why I could not have one day off for rest.

I am a busy mum with three kids, I work, I write, I do ministry, I run a business, I run a non-profit, I am a prayer minister...I, I, and more I. I thought I had some great excuses until God reminded me through Scripture that he

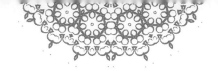

created the WHOLE UNIVERSE in six days and still maintains and looks after everything that concerns us today. I AM NOT SO BUSY that I cannot rest in Him.

God created us in His image, and if He needed a day off from work, so do we. God was so passionate about our need to rest that He didn't make it a suggestion; He didn't even make it optional, like a *"do it if you like"* kind of idea. No, He made it a commandment, a must. Why? Because it is important that we rest. But He didn't only make it a day to rest; He made it a blessed and holy day of rest.

The Bible tells us in Exodus 20:8–11 ESV, *"Remember the Sabbath day, to keep it holy. Six days you shall labor, and do all your work, but the seventh day is a Sabbath to the Lord your God. On it you shall not do any work, you, or your son, or your daughter, your male servant, or your female servant, or your livestock, or the sojourner who is within your gates. For in six days the Lord made heaven and earth, the sea, and all that is in them, and rested on the seventh day. Therefore the Lord blessed the Sabbath day and made it holy."*

I love the way the verse starts with the word 'remember', because we can easily get caught up with activities in life such that we forget the Sabbath rest, a holy day set aside by God for us to rest in Him and draw the strength that we

need to face and overcome the challenges of life.

We should have one day when we can shut down from all the stress, work, and troubles of life and just focus on Him. God is our source, it is His air that we breathe; He is the one who keeps us alive and well, and we need Him to survive.

There is nothing the devil likes more than a tired Christian. The devil wants you to live a stress-filled life because he knows that when you are tired, you are weak, not just in body but in spirit, and you become easy prey. The devil will look for ways through work and other necessary activities to keep us busy constantly so that we don't have time to rest.

As women of God, we need to actively choose to rest. We need to rest as though it is a weapon, like it is our battle cry. I am not talking about extra sleep, going on a holiday, or reducing your hours at work. I am talking about making a conscious decision to set aside one day that is focused on spending time with God and doing NO WORK at all.

Earlier, I talked about the Israelites and the daily provision of manna. There was only one exception to that rule of daily manna, and that was the day before the Sabbath. The Bible tells us an exciting story in Exodus 16 of how God provided food for His children.

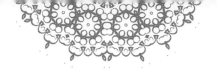

For five days, they could only gather enough for the day—the ones who tried to gather extra woke up to maggots and a foul odour the next day—but on the sixth day, they were able to gather food for two days, so they didn't need to do any work on the Sabbath day but to keep it holy.

Exodus 16:23 NLT says,
"He told them, 'This is what the Lord commanded: Tomorrow will be a day of complete rest, a holy Sabbath day set apart for the Lord. So bake or boil as much as you want today, and set aside what is left for tomorrow."

This was how much God put importance on this day of rest; He didn't even want them to come out of their houses to pick up food to eat. He wanted them to stay indoors and just rest. We need to go back to the source for strength or we will end up unable to cope with life and we will instead live in distress.

If you are hesitant about this habit, you are in good company. Trust me, I was too, but God had to teach me in practical ways that this luxury of the Sabbath rest that I couldn't afford to do was the one thing that I couldn't afford not to do. It was for my good and His glory.

I grew up using a manual toothbrush and continued to use one well into my 30s. I started having a lot of problems with my teeth: My mouth was very sensitive, my gums were bleeding at times, and I was so worried that something was wrong. Anyway, I went to the dentist, who after an oral examination told me I had cavities, I needed a root canal, I needed a broken wisdom tooth extracted, and I also had early signs of gum disease. I was shocked and upset. He recommended I start to use an electric toothbrush instead, so I got one.

I am one of those people who just take things out of the box and figures them out; I don't like instruction manuals much, so I didn't learn how to use it; I just started using it.

A few months later, I went back to the dentist for a check-up, and there was very little improvement. He and I were both surprised, and I was slightly disappointed. I sat there wondering, what was I doing wrong? I had spent so much money on this Oral B fancy toothbrush—and yet nothing. He then asked me to show him how I used my electric toothbrush, and I did. He laughed.

I was using my electric toothbrush in the same way I used a manual toothbrush, which basically defeated the whole purpose of an electric toothbrush. He told me that with an electric toothbrush, I really didn't need to do anything; all I needed to do was to put in on my teeth and gums and move it around my mouth seconds apart and that the toothbrush does all the work. I didn't need to use my strength to brush my teeth; I just needed to position the

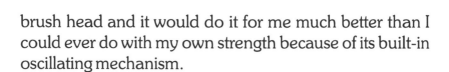

brush head and it would do it for me much better than I could ever do with my own strength because of its built-in oscillating mechanism.

Later that day, God showed me that it is a great example of how His grace works, that when we try to live our lives like a manual toothbrush with our own wisdom and strength, we can only accomplish a little.

We have areas in our lives that become exposed and liable to gum disease, but if we just allow Him to be Lord of our lives and be in control, like an electric toothbrush, He will do all the work. All we had to do was position Him and give Him permission to touch the areas of our lives that need His cleansing touch, healing, redemption, deliverance, or whatever we need, and He will do it effectively.

God used my own story to teach me that all our life struggles can be solved if we simply make the switch from manual to electric, to move from human to Holy Spirit.

However, I learnt the hard way about the importance of plugging back into the source one day as I brushed my teeth and the battery ran out halfway through. If you have an electric toothbrush, I am sure you will agree that there is nothing as annoying as or more useless than an electric toothbrush with no power. The bristles are so soft that you can't get your teeth cleaned without power. Unlike a manual toothbrush that is built to give some effect without power, the electric toothbrush without power cannot work as effectively as a manual toothbrush. It needs to be plugged back into the source to charge, and it takes hours to charge fully.

That is what the Sabbath rest in God is about—taking that one day to get our spirit plugged back into God's spirit to charge effectively so that we have the strength to deal with the other six days in the week. We need time to fully reconnect with God in an uninterrupted and continuous charge.

I know that this may be a hard habit to learn or even to understand and appreciate, but know that you will be more effective in your six days of work if you give your seventh day to God.

When we work under grace, we are equipped with wisdom that helps us work smart not hard. Think about the story of King David and Goliath. Many people had tried and failed to kill goliath using their own strength and weapons, yet, David killed him with one stone and a slingshot; that is the type of wisdom that comes out of resting in God.

If you are a woman who does that bit extra, you work a full-time job with some business on the side, or you have other interests that keep you busy, ask God to show you how to do it all in six days, and He will. He will bless you with divine wisdom, knowledge, strength and much more. You will see how much richer your life will become if for just one day in the week you are plugged into God and family life only.

Keeping the Sabbath day holy is an Old Testament commandment, and you can argue that we are no longer under the law but under grace, however, personally, I take the view that if I can honour God with one day and walk in His example, then He will surely bless the other six days.

However, the Sabbath is not just an old commandment, Jesus taught us about the Sabbath in the New Testament in Matthew 12:1–14. The Pharisees were trying to trap Jesus by legalising the Sabbath, but I love how Jesus showed us that the Sabbath rest was not limited to the law or being observed as a religious activity; it doesn't excuse us from doing good things.

Please don't get worried and think that you cannot help people on your day of rest or prepare food to eat or anything like that. No, the Bible tells us in

Mark 2:27 NLT,
"Then Jesus said to them, 'The Sabbath was made to meet the needs of people, and not people to meet the requirements of the Sabbath.'"

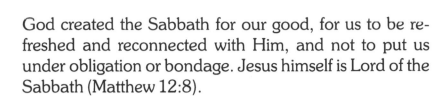

God created the Sabbath for our good, for us to be refreshed and reconnected with Him, and not to put us under obligation or bondage. Jesus himself is Lord of the Sabbath (Matthew 12:8).

To be honest, I didn't immediately start to observe the Sabbath rest. I still had my excuses. Yes, God had been speaking to me about it; I had been doing research, asking questions, and trying to decide what day would be my seventh day. How will I begin, what am I supposed to do, and all those questions kept me from making the decision to just start and focus on resting in God, but then I found

Hebrews 4:9–11:
"There remains, then, a Sabbath-rest for the people of God; for anyone who enters God's rest also rests from their works, just as God did from His. Let us, therefore, make every effort to enter that rest, so that no one will perish by following their example of disobedience."
(Emphasis mine)

What God showed me through that scripture is that the Sabbath rest was not just an Old Testament commandment and that there are consequences from not entering His rest. As women of God who want to build resilience and have the strength to live life to the fullest, we need to enter His rest. The Bible says in the scripture above that we should *"make every effort to enter that rest"* so that we

don't perish because of our disobedience.

It's going to be hard work; the devil won't just sit there and say, *"Yeah, go and rest, woman."* We need to fight for our rest as though our lives depend on it because the truth is, IT DOES. Our lives depend on our ability to rest in God because He is our source; He is where it all starts and ends. He is where we draw true strength from. Rest should not be a last option; it should be the first—the Bible says we should SEEK HIM FIRST.

God showed me that a lot of the sickness in this world today, especially mental health issues, is out of a direct disobedience to not having a rest in Him, not because He is a wicked God and is punishing us for not resting but because when we don't rest in Him and connect with Him, we open the door for the devil to come in and cause havoc in our lives that we are not spiritually equipped to fight without God.

Therefore, the devil likes to keep us busy, tired, stressed, and overwhelmed—so that we don't find time to rest in God. The devil knows that we need that day to reconnect with God. We need that time to be in God's presence, so he will do anything that he can, to prevent us from resting in God.

We must know that we, too, were created to work for six days and rest on the seventh day as well. It is very important. It is not something we need to fit into our lifestyle; it is something we fit our lifestyle into. I encourage you to go to God in prayer and ask him to reveal His heart to you concerning the Sabbath rest. Ask Him to teach you what you need to learn, and take some time to do some more research if you feel the need to.

REST is such an important habit to learn if you want to build resilience and if you truly want to make strength a lifestyle. Rest is a weapon you can use to fight adversity. It is not about being lazy, so don't let the devil deceive you with false guilt. I carried this for many years as well, thinking, how can I rest when I should be doing this or that? I now know that I need to rest so I can effectively do this and that.

If you don't make rest a priority through wilful choice, your body will make it a priority for you through stress, anxiety, depression, sickness, and disease. You could open yourself to the possibility of living a life filled with guilt, anxiety, and regret because when you make choices in a state of unrest, you make choices that will negatively affect you.

A tired Christian is a prey for the enemy, and he will always be ready to take advantage of a willing prey. Yes, he is a coward like that and he takes delight in deepening the cuts of the wounded. He will pounce when he finds you outside God's rest.

Our ability to be resilient; our true strength, comes out of our purposeful rest in God.

Isaiah 40:30-31 NKJV says,
"Even the youths shall faint and be weary, And the young men shall utterly fall, But those who wait on the Lord Shall renew their strength; They shall mount up with wings like eagles, They shall run and not be weary, They shall walk and not faint."

SABBATH TIP

Don't bring the Law into your Sabbath rest. It doesn't have to be any specific day. Just make it your seventh day, and choose not to do ANY WORK. No checking work emails, no work or business conversations, and nothing that signifies any kind of work. Just Rest. Worship. Pray. Fellowship.

Ask God how best to use that day and what He wants your Sabbath rest to be. Let it be between you and God because this is not a religious exercise, it should be a relationship based on love with your heavenly Father, a time to reconnect. If you are in ministry and you have to teach or pray, do good things—don't use the Sabbath as an excuse not to do God's work—however, don't use it as an excuse to work either. Also, don't limit your presence in God to just your Sabbath day; you still need to live in the present with Him daily. If you feel you cannot afford to

rest, pause and think, CAN YOU REALLY AFFORD NOT TO?

I encourage you to pause and take the time to do the exercises at the end of this chapter as they will help you on your journey to becoming a resilient woman of God. Don't overlook this step and jump right in to the next chapter. Take the time to work through these questions, and to pray.

I am privileged to share God's truths with you, but it is my desire that you get a personal revelation from each chapter for yourself. Ask God to teach you what He wants you to learn from each chapter, and make notes that you can refer to over and over again. Don't just read this book; make it your personal journal for a personal journey. Work through it, and watch God work through you.

Let's Pray

Dear Father,
thank you that You love me so much that You want me to
draw all my strength, wisdom, and purpose from You.
Thank you for the cross that tore down the veil of separation
and restored my relationship with You. Now I can come into
your presence through Jesus, who is the way for us all. I
pray, Lord, that You teach me the importance of the Sab-
bath rest and show me how and when to rest in You. I pray
that as I come to You to rest that my mind, body, and spirit
would be healed and that You would fill me with all the
resources and wisdom that I need to do much more in six
days than I could have ever accomplished in seven days.
In Jesus' name, Amen.

Write your own prayers

....

....

....

....

Workbook 5

Reflections on Habit 4

Strength through REST in God

Q1 What has struck you most about this chapter?

....
....
....
....
....
....

Q2 Read Hebrews 4:9—11, and meditate on it. What is God saying to you?

....
....
....
....
....
....

Q3 Why is it important to you to enter God's rest?

....
....
....
....
....

Q4 What are the things that you think will prevent you from having a Sabbath rest?

....

....

....

....

....

....

Q5 What things can you do to remove the challenges so that you can have your Sabbath rest?

....

....

....

....

....

....

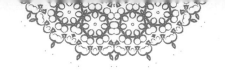

Find and write out scriptures that will encourage you on this habit

....

....

....

....

....

....

....

....

....

....

....

....

....

....

....

....

....

....

Notes

....
....
....
....
....
....
....
....
....
....
....
....
....
....
....
....
....
....

HABIT 5

Stories That EMPOWER and INSPIRE

"Let all that I am praise the LORD;
may I never forget the good things he
does for me."
Psalm 103:2 NLT

HABIT 5

Telling your story gives you strength. You are reminded of your victory in adversity and empowered to live life knowing what you have overcome before and what you can overcome again. Your story also inspires other people not to give up, to have faith, and to keeping standing firm through their own challenges in life.

I have many stories to tell of what God has done in my life, and I believe that as I grow and do life with God, there will be many more stories to tell. In my first book, *The Love That Set Me Free*, which I wrote over three years and first published in 2016, I shared my story of triumph over a childhood of sexual abuse and how God's love was the foundation for the freedom and healing I enjoy today.

God has done much more; He has brought me through a lot more. At the time, I was going through the challenges of life, they seemed painful and pointless, but as I look back, I can see God's hand. It is now obvious why He allowed certain things to happen, and how those things have shaped me and made me into the woman I am today. I want to share a brief and very summarised story of my journey into motherhood knowing that it will

inspire you and empower me. Sometimes, we need to hear other people's stories, so that we would realise that we are not alone. We are not isolated in our struggles.

My childhood of painful abuse is the root cause of many of the challenges I suffered growing up. I was filled with low self-esteem and self-hate, and I had many negative beliefs and mindsets about myself. It was these same beliefs that I carried into my matrimonial home and they served as a dysfunctional foundation for my journey to motherhood.

I got pregnant with my first son, Joshua, while I was still in university. I was very excited, and so was his dad – we decided to get married and start life together. I thought that having my own family would finally give me the joy I so eagerly craved, that I would have the life I dreamed about and the love that I so desperately needed in my life.

I am not sure where or how I formed this opinion, but somewhere deep on the inside of me, I believed that when I had my own children, they would love me uncon-ditionally, they would not judge me, they would not know anything about my shameful past, and that it would all be a bed of roses. So, my journey into motherhood started on the premise that I would have the unconditional love I needed from my children.

My pregnancy was difficult during the latter stages, and I

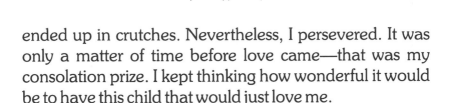

ended up in crutches. Nevertheless, I persevered. It was only a matter of time before love came—that was my consolation prize. I kept thinking how wonderful it would be to have this child that would just love me.

The labour was a long 19.5 hours, and the delivery was one that can only be described as horror. It was traumatic. I finally gave birth to my son via forceps. I took one look at him, and my first impression was not love. Yes, I was happy that he was finally here, he was well and cute, yet, I didn't feel that connection that I expected. I cried, but they were not tears of joy—they were tears of not being able to feel joy. What was wrong with me? Why wasn't I happy? I always felt I was abnormal somehow, and the emotions that went through me that day confirmed my worst fears. What type of mother was not smitten with her child's arrival?

I felt very dirty and uncomfortable, not just from child-birth but internally as well. Somehow, I felt defiled. I wanted to be alone and just cry, weep from my soul with the disappointment of not being able to bond with my son and the guilt that overwhelmed me. I neglected my mother-in-law's advice to just rest and decided to go and have a shower instead. My husband decided to come with me, to my initial annoyance, yet it was a blessing because less than two minutes after I stepped into the shower, the world began to spin around me, and I passed out in the shower.

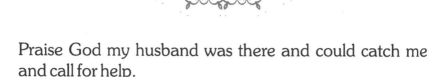

Praise God my husband was there and could catch me and call for help.

I had third degree tears and was in agony for days. My stiches and womb became infected, my breasts were infected, and everything was just plain hard and sore. This was not at all what I had bargained for. You see, what I did not realise nor understand before my fairy-tale journey into motherhood was that I needed to love my baby too, that the descending love needs to be greater than the ascending love, that I had the responsibility to love this child first and take care of his needs. This was nothing like playing with a dolly—this was real life.

But how do you give something you don't have? I know the Bible says we should love our neighbour like we love ourselves—that's the great commandment, one that I grew up knowing so well—yet how do you live to the fullness of that commandment if one bit of the equation is broken? How could I love my son when I hated myself?

What I thought would be a joy just as I had imagined, quickly became a massive mountain in the dark—a mountain so big yet, I had to climb it feeling powerless and unable to begin.

Because my womb was infected, and prolapsed, I had several consultant appointments. At one of them, a scan revealed that I had fibroids coupled with some other complications. My husband and I were basically told we could not have any more children, yet three months later, to our huge surprise, I was pregnant with our second child.

My second labour came with similar challenges. This time I was induced a week earlier as a precaution because of the trauma from my previous birth. It was a shorter labour, it was planned, and it was a more straightforward birth, but still, I had third degree vaginal tears and I had yet another baby wanting me to love him. Wanting something I didn't have in me to give.

It was easy to love my husband or, so I thought. I equated sex with love, and I could give that. I had gotten away without loving in the true sense by just exchanging my body as the prize instead. Yes, I did experience some moments of happiness, and I thought how I behaved was love - or at least a kind of love. However, to love my children required something more, something deeper, and something I didn't understand.

Those first two years of motherhood were extremely hard, and I walked them in tears and agony. I cried most days and nights; I cried as the children cried. I was tired, frustrated, and very unhappy. I didn't know what to do or how to cope, as I struggled with intense emotions. I finally got to the end of myself one day and thought I couldn't do it anymore when God sent an angel in the form of a health visitor. It was she who encouraged me to speak with my GP, who finally put me on medication for post-natal depression.

The thought of being a bad mother filled my existence for many, many years. I couldn't trust myself to be alone for an extended period with my own children. It wasn't just that I didn't know how but that I didn't want to be. It took too much out of me. Motherhood was my weakness, and I internalised it. I was ashamed, I felt so guilty and I thought it was just me. I was around other people who seemed to be doing a pretty good job.

In those days, women were not as transparent with their challenges as today; everyone went about as though they were super mum, and so did I. No one knew how much I was hurting, how incapable I felt, how much I was crying each night.

I covered up my inadequacy with work, and I went back to work as quickly as I could after each pregnancy. I also had help, from childminders to live-in au pairs, to fam-ily—I made sure there was constantly someone else involved in my childcare duties whether I needed it or not. I couldn't understand why life was so bitter for me, why I didn't have any confidence, self-esteem, hated myself, and why I made all the wrong choices that I did.

Things only started making sense the year I turned 28 –

when I remembered my abuse and started to understand the effects. I was already a wife and a mother, and had to deal with the memories as well as everything else going on; it was no surprise that my marriage was hanging on to God for its dear life, and I was on the verge of another emotional breakdown. Yet somehow God kept me.

We moved from London to Kent, and life continued as best as it could. It was in 2012 that I first heard God call me into my role of full time motherhood. By this time, I had three children, and I was doing a job that I enjoyed and earning more money than I ever had. We had both our older boys at an independent school, and my daughter was in nursery. Life seemed okay on the outside, but I was still very broken on the inside.

I had done a lot of counselling, and my journey towards healing was going great. I had started writing my book, and life seemed a bit stable. It took me a while, but I finally gave up my job in London. I had enough money saved up such that I could focus on the kids, but a few weeks in, I panicked. I just couldn't do it, so I got a live-in au pair, got another job, and went back to work.

Again, in 2014, God called me to be home and to just be a mum, and again I quit my job only to get another au pair and go back to work. When that au pair ran away with our money and gifts close to Christmas, we decided not to have live-in au pairs but live-out nannies instead.

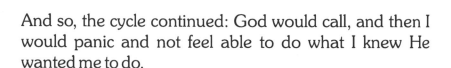

And so, the cycle continued: God would call, and then I would panic and not feel able to do what I knew He wanted me to do.

By 2016, I was out of work again, but this time it was different. I was broke. We were in the process of selling a property that had been on the market for a long time and were having to maintain the mortgage and bills on two properties.

We needed to do this to protect our credit rating so that we could eventually buy another house when we sold the old one. I was out of work, and as Easter approached, for the first time, I knew that I was going to have to look after the children myself. I had no money to pay for childcare and no money to send them to holiday club. For the first time ever, I was stuck with the kids.

It was like God took everything away, such that I had nothing but me and my mountain, and because I had nothing else but God, I had nothing else I could do but turn to God. I couldn't go and borrow money to send my kids to holiday club because I felt unable to be a mum! I was home, I wasn't working, so what would have been my excuse?

Fear gripped me, and I went into panic mode. I was literally out of my comfort zone already by getting them up, getting them ready for school in one piece, bringing

them home again, feeding them, bathing them, and sending them off to bed and still being sane. At this stage, my kids were 11, 10, and 6, and this was the first time I had full responsibility for them.

I don't know if any mums can relate to this, but every morning in my house was a battle. The boys would fight about such insignificant things like, *"He looked at me funny"*, breakfast was a war zone, and who sat in the front seat was another reason for a battle. Lost water bottles and school stuff, homework, and after school activities…it seemed endless, yet I knew that there were six hours in a day when I could have some time to cry in peace. And yes, many, many days were filled with tears. I felt so inadequate, but I hid it well.

Easter holidays approached…how would I cope? I started praying. Each morning I was praying, trusting God for His grace, praying that He would give me the heart to love my children. Then God showed me that it was not about them but about me. He said motherhood was less about what I needed to do but more about who he needed me to become.

He showed me that it was not they who needed to change but it was I who needed to change. My children were not listening to me; they were watching me. As a mother, I train by example, not by words, and my actions are much more important than what I could ever say. God also

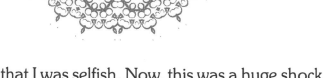

showed me that I was selfish. Now, this was a huge shock to me. If I could describe myself, selfish would not be the word I would use.

I always thought of myself as selfless, always willing to help, always going out of my way for people. God showed me that I was selfish with my time. I was always willing to give away money, but my time, now that was different. And children spelled love with time. They didn't want anything else from me; they just wanted me. They just wanted their mum, and I felt so hurt and broken and not in tune with who I was that I was not willing to give them me.

I never thought that I was enough. I was afraid that if they got too close or knew who I really was, they would see through me and not love me. It was such a fragile place to be, and now that I look back, it feels irrational, but behind my selfishness was fear and pride. God wanted to heal that.

God was more interested in changing me than he was in changing my circumstances. Even when I prayed for a job and for the house to sell quickly so that we could have the money we needed, God seemed silent. I used to wonder where God was amid my adversity, but now I realise how he used that period to train me.

I started to live every day with God, and it was hard. I

prayed for God to turn me into the Proverbs 31 woman. By this time, I had accepted that this was something I needed to do, and there was no going back. I had to be a mum and raise my kids, but I wanted to do it the Proverbs 31 way. This was my prayer for days and days until one-day God said, "Amanda, you need to learn how to be a 1 Corinthians 13 mother first. It all starts with love."

1 Corinthians 13:4–7 NLT says,
"Love is patient and kind. Love is not jealous or boast-ful or proud or rude. It does not demand its own way. It is not irritable, and it keeps no record of being wronged. It does not rejoice about injustice but rejoices whenever the truth wins out. Love never gives up, never loses faith, is always hopeful, and endures through every circumstance."

God needed me to see His love towards me; that He was patient with me, He was kind...He was all of that and more, never giving up on me. He showed me His fatherly heart and started to breathe His love into me so that I could pour out to my children.

God knew I didn't have all the love I needed of myself to give to them, but He gave me His love and filled me so much, that I was able to learn to love my kids through Him. I am no longer a woman threatened by the Proverbs 31 woman, I have become a woman who is learning the importance of love.

Maybe motherhood came naturally to you, but for me, it was a difficult journey, and I learnt it through God. I learnt it through such heavy dependence on Him. I was home for 18 months, and by His grace, motherhood flowed through me. Easter was hard, summer was easier, and by Easter of the next year, I was a semi - professional mum.

Now looking after my kids, the thing that was such a mountain, has become a stepping stone. God used what was an adversity to grow me, to change me, and to make me a better person. My life is so much richer; I have a taste of the love I craved. But it also impacted other areas of my life, my marriage, my friendships and even my relationship with myself.

Yes, I still have my days, and yes, I still cry—but mainly because I am hormonal. And yes, my children still crawl up my back and make me want to pull my eyes out, BUT I can do all things through Jesus, who has given me strength. I have both my boys in grammar school and my little angel just starting prep school, and I know that it is all by God's grace and goodness.

There is a lot more to the story and I will share some valuable lessons that I have learnt in a book one day soon, but for now, I want you to know that because my past didn't kill me like I thought it would; because I didn't fail like I thought I would, I have the opportunity to share this story with you. It is not an easy story to share, but I pray that it inspires you as you read it and that it helps you know that God is in the middle of everything that you are going through and He has a good plan. It may look like nothing good can come out of that difficult situation, but just trust God. He is in control. He makes no mistakes.

When I sit down and think of all that God has brought me through, all I have overcome by His grace, I am empowered. I know that if He could do that for me, He will do much more. My life's stories empower me to dream big, to hope in God, to have faith, and to never give up.

Share your story—let it empower you and inspire others. No story is too big or too small. You never know who needs to hear what you have to say. Our testimonies are a reminder for us and an inspiration to others. They help us to build resilience, to be strong women. We see how God, who did it yesterday, will do it for us today and tomorrow, and we can relax in His goodness.

Our testimonies will bring healing to other people and will help us be witnesses to others of the great God we serve. People can discount what the Bible says, but no one can discount your personal story. You are able to say, *"I believe in God, and I know He is real. Let me tell you what He did for me…"* with this you can lead people to the cross and, by God's grace, bring them to repentance. You can bring hope into a hopeless world. Your story is so vital in this world today.

No one can dispute the power of God in your own life and the word of your testimony. You don't need to be a pastor or a Bible teacher, and you don't even need a theology degree to be a witness for God; you just need to tell someone what God has done for you and see the impact it will make in their lives. The Bible teaches us in John 4 about the importance of telling our story. The chapter talks about Jesus' conversation with the Samaritan woman and the impact it had in her life. The impact is evident in her response as she ran into her town to tell her story. The Bible then tells us in

John 4:39 NKJV,
"And many of the Samaritans of that city believed in Him because of the word of the woman who testified, 'He told me all that I ever did.'"

Many people believed in Jesus just from the word of her testimony. Again, in John 9, the Bible tells us the story of the blind man. The Pharisees were interrogating him about his healing and what happened, and they went as far as interrogating his parents about his miracle, but his explanation to them in verse 25 was simple and impactful: *"But I know this: I was blind, and now I can see!"*

All we need to do with our story is to tell it as best as we can. The things that happen to us are for our good, and they bring glory to God. Our story helps us spread God's glory. The word *"testimony"* has its roots in the words *"witness"*, which in its root meaning means to do again, to repeat, to do over. So, in other words, sharing our testimony releases God's power *"to do again"*.

We limit God when we don't share our testimony, when we don't tell of the good things he has done.
The Bible says in

Psalm 78:40–42 NKJV,
"How often they provoked Him in the wilderness, And grieved Him in the desert! Yes, again and again they tempted God, And limited the Holy One of Israel. They did not remember His power: The day when He re-deemed them from the enemy."

By sharing our story, we remember God and what he has done, we give him thanks, and we sow seeds of faith and goodness. The more we tell our story, the more we will have stories to tell.

The devil is always there looking for ways to destroy us. The Bible says day and night he is like a busybody pointing his finger, basically saying, *"Look at your children. Look what they did."* But I love what the Bible says in

Revelation 12:10–11 NKJV:
"Then I heard a loud voice saying in heaven, "Now salvation, and strength,

and the kingdom of our God, and the power of His Christ have come, for the accuser of our brethren, who accused them before our God day and night, has been cast down.
11 And they overcame him by the blood of the Lamb and by the word of their testimony, and they did not love their lives to the death."

The Bible says that salvation and strength have come to us in Jesus' name and that the devil has been cast out because we have overcome him by the blood of the Lamb and the word of our testimony. Don't ever underestimate the power in your testimony. It brings life, it brings salvation, it gives strength, and it defeats the enemy.

❧ HOW TO TELL YOUR STORY

You can tell your story in many ways. You can share it face-to-face with friends, colleagues, and family. You can write it and share it on social media. You can give a testimony in church, or you can even make a video about your story.

However, you share your story, remember one thing: Let it honour God. Someone asked me, *"How can you share your story without coming across like you are boasting?"* It's such a great question. I believe that when you share your story in a way that shows things worked out for your good and give glory to God, then you are boasting about

God's goodness in your life, and that is a wonderful thing.

Remember, your story is powerful. It casts down the devil, and it shuts him up. It gives glory to God, and it empowers you and inspires others.

I encourage you to pause and take the time to do the exercises at the end of this chapter as they will help you on your journey to becoming a resilient woman of God. Don't overlook this step and jump right in to the next chapter. Take the time to work through these questions, and take the time to pray.

I am privileged to share God's truths with you, but it is my desire that you get a personal revelation from each chapter for yourself. Ask God to teach you personally what He wants you to learn from each chapter, and make notes that you can refer to over and over again. Don't just read this book; make it your personal journal for a personal journey. Work through it, and watch God work through you.

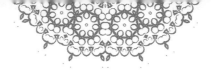

Let's Pray

Dear Father,
thank you for everything You have done in my life, for
where You have brought me from, and where You are taking
me to. Lord, I want to honour You with my story. I want to
tell of all the good things You have done for me, from the
small things to the big things. Please, Lord, give me the
courage to share my story, and bless me with the opportuni-
ties to tell of Your goodness. I invite You to come and
continue the good work You have started in my life and to
give me many more stories to tell.
In Jesus' name, Amen.

Write your own prayers

....

....

....

....

....

Reflections on Habit 5

Stories That EMPOWER and INSPIRE

Q1 What has struck you most about this chapter?

....

....

....

....

....

....

Q2 Read 1 Corinthians 13:4–7, and meditate on it. In what ways can you learn to love?

....

....

....

....

....

....

Q3 Write a list of your stories, and remember what God has done for you.

....

....

....

....

....

....

Q4 Write a list of people that you will share your stories with.

....

....

....

....

....

....

Q5 In what ways will you share your story?

....

....

....

....

....

....

Find and write out scriptures that will encourage you on this habit

....
....
....
....
....
....
....
....
....
....
....
....
....
....
....
....
....
....

Notes

....
....
....
....
....
....
....
....
....
....
....
....
....
....
....
....
....
....

CONCLUSION

I thank you for taking time to read this book, for welcoming my words into your mind and allowing God to minister to your heart. It's been an awesome privilege to share my heart with you.

I may not have told you anything new. The habits I've shared in this book are things you may have heard before. However, I believe that by God's grace, I have been able to give you a fresh and renewed perspective in a way that enables you to understand them and inspires you to try to incorporate these habits into your life.

You really can make strength a lifestyle if you take the time to put into practice what you have read. I hope that you have worked through the chapter reflections and will put into practice all you have learnt.

I know it's not going to be easy. I'm still on the journey myself—a lifelong habit that becomes a lifestyle is not formed overnight. I don't believe it takes 21–30 days either; I believe it takes much longer, and new research shows this to be true. So, give yourself some grace. Don't try to do it all at once.

My desire is to teach you what I've learnt but then to point you back to Jesus for direction. I encourage you to take

time to pray about each habit and to ask God to speak to you specifically. I know that He has a blessing in store for you, and I am so excited to be a small part of your journey.

♪ HEAVEN'S CALL

Do you know Jesus as your personal Lord and Saviour? Have you accepted Him into your life? Do you need to rediscover your relationship with God? It is not too late to be welcomed into God's family. Jesus loves you so much and wants to walk with you in every area of your life, but you need to make a choice to give your life to Him. I promise you, He will protect your life, cherish you, and bless you in ways you never dreamed possible. All you have to do is ask Him to come in.

The Bible says in

Revelation 3:20 NLT,
"Look! I stand at the door and knock. If you hear my voice and open the door, I will come in, and we will share a meal together as friends."

Let's Pray

Dear Jesus, I thank you for loving me so much. I invite you today into my heart. I welcome You to come and be my Lord and my Saviour, to be the Lord over every area of my life. I don't know where this journey will lead me, but I know that I can rest safely in your arms. I want to be a woman of faith and purpose. I want to serve you, Lord, and I pray that my life will be a testimony of your goodness. Thank you for choosing me.
In Jesus' name, Amen.

I am privileged to welcome you into God's family. I would love to hear from you. It would be an honour to know how this book has impacted you and the steps you are taking to become a more resilient woman of God, making strength a lifestyle. Yes, you can.

Write your own prayers

....

....

....

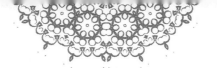

*If you would like to share your story with me,
please send an email to*

info@activatetherealyou.com

*I look forward to hearing from you.
God bless you. Amen.*

About The Author

Amanda is a wife and a mother to three beautiful children. She is an author, a prayer minister, an inspirational speaker, a restoration catalyst, a coach, and a mentor. Amanda is passionate about seeing people restored and living a full life beyond salvation.

She is a passionate Bible teacher who uses practical examples to teach godly principles. She is a Law Graduate (LLBs Hons) from the University of Wolverhampton, a Prince 2 Practitioner, and is certified in Business Analysis Practice.

She is the founder of 'Activate the Real You', an organisation that has been set up with the mission "To point Christians to Jesus so that He can Rebuild, Repair, and Revive those who are hurting and broken-hearted. To help Christians rediscover their identity in Jesus so that they can be restored and live a life of purpose, becoming true disciples of Jesus Christ".

Visit www.activatetherealyou.com

Amanda is also the founder and CEO of Empower a Woman (www.empowerawoman.org), a UK-based non-profit organisation that is set up to meet the needs of vulnerable women.

Her dream is to create a platform where women who are serious about making positive changes in their lives, have the opportunity to do so. Her passion stems out of her own life experiences. She was sexually abused as a child by some close family members and has faced great adversity in her life.

Today, she is in a much happier place. She is restored, healed, and delivered and is driven by her own personal mission statement for change:

> *Just because I can't do everything*
> *Doesn't mean I won't do anything*
> *Even if I can only do something*
> *I REFUSE to do nothing*

ACTIVATE THE REAL YOU

I saw my brother's dead body when I was only twelve years old. He was my best friend and my hero. I was with him moments before he died, and when I heard he had died in the hospital, I ran all the way there and uncovered his dead body. I had to see him for myself to believe it. His death introduced my little heart to an inexplicable pain. I was broken, and I was afraid.

At 28, I remembered I was sexually abused as a child. That was just one of the many traumatic things I had faced in life. Before then, my life was a roller coaster of pain, trauma, and bad choices. I had been saved and re-saved many times; I would give my life to Jesus and try to live a righteous life, but I would backslide so often that it felt like I was in a dance with my salvation. It was very frustrating to know what to do, to desperately want to do it, but to not be able to do it.

I lived a life of shame, guilt, regret, and depression. How could I be saved and still be so broken? Where was Jesus? Wasn't my salvation enough? I often asked myself these questions.

In 2012, I was in a women's meeting organised by my local church and I heard a lady read out Psalm 139 with such a poetic voice; every word flowed out like a musical note. It was very beautiful. It was the beginning of my restoration journey. It was then I truly realised God's fatherly heart towards me, that I was not a mistake and that I was an important part of this world.

I rededicated my life to Jesus in that meeting, but this time it was different. All my life I had lived under religion, plagued with the rules of what was and wasn't acceptable. I had a very limited understanding of God's grace, and I never truly knew what it meant to have a personal, intimate, one-on-one relationship with my Saviour. Something changed in me that night, and I went home filled with joy and excited for the journey ahead.

Now, I was married with three children, and I was on medication for depression. The year before, I'd had a mental breakdown, and life was very complicated. I left that meeting believing for a complete change. I was saved again, and this time it was for good.

It was a huge SHOCK to me when I found myself again faced with my past sins in my present state. I had tried to put new wine into old wineskins, and of course there were leaks and tears. Again, frustration set in, and the same old voices screamed, "You are never going to change!"
I felt like a failure because I had tried to change many times in my own strength, and here I was trying to change again, but I couldn't. Wasn't my salvation enough? Wasn't I truly saved?

I worked in the NHS at the time, and it seemed the new buzz word was TRANSFORMATION. Everybody was doing something or the other that had to do with transformation, and I, too, was very desperate to transform my life, but I couldn't. I failed miserably. There's a certain kind of inner bitterness that plagues you when you think you are not good enough, and yet still you cannot even pretend to be someone else. How could I be so useless at being me and even worse at being them?

The truth that took me years to discover is simply this: God didn't want me to become someone else; He wanted me to become ME—the person He created as His original masterpiece. The words in Psalm 139:13–18 suddenly became true in my life, and I realised why I had connected with it so much in that meeting in 2012.

So instead of going on a journey of TRANSFORMATION, God took me on a journey of RESTORATION. God took me apart and put me back together again. It was painful, and it was slow, but I didn't do that journey alone. God blessed me with key people and organisations, and He loved the hurt away. By His grace, I was restored to wholeness; I discovered who I truly was in Jesus, and I am currently living out my purpose.

I always wanted to know why I had failed and fallen so many times. God showed me that not only was I on the wrong journey by trying to be transformed, instead of being restored, but I had never fully progressed beyond my salvation.

Jesus sent His disciples into the world not just to preach the gospel, so that people can be saved but to heal the sick and cast out demons. What I needed after being saved was to be healed and delivered, but I didn't know that. I wasn't taught that. I thought my salvation was enough and that Jesus would wave a magic wand and all would be okay. There was so much more I needed to do and learn beyond saying I DO to Jesus.

Now that I am saved, healed, delivered, and restored, my life is very different. Yes, I still have some challenges, and life is not filled with roses, but I have learnt what it means to trust God, to have faith and the power of forgiveness. I have the FULL ARMOUR of God, and I am not afraid to use it.

Isaiah 61:1 (NLT) is a very popular scripture that says, *"The Spirit of the Sovereign Lord is upon me, for the Lord has anointed me to bring good news to the poor. He has sent me to comfort the broken-hearted and to proclaim that captives will be released and prisoners will be freed."*

Yet my own story can be found in Isaiah 61:4 NLT: *"They will rebuild the ancient ruins, repairing cities destroyed long ago. They will revive them, though they have been deserted for many generations."*

I used to be a hurting and broken person, but I was

healed, delivered, and completely restored by God's grace. I am now on a mission to rebuild, repair, and revive God's children who are broken and hurting like I was. I am very passionate about seeing God's children live to their fullest potential and not be held captive by the trauma in their past, their mistakes, broken hearts, or anything else. It is for our freedom that Jesus died, and we must live in the fullness of the cross.

It's been a long but interesting journey for me, and I have learnt so many things along the way that I would love to share with you. I welcome you to join the Activate the Real You community, where there are a lot of free services that would help you on your journey.

Because the distance between brokenness and restoration is blood, sweat, and tears...you will need good company.
Don't travel alone.

Join us.
www.activatetherealyou.com

Amanda Bedzrah.

Books by Amanda Bedzrah

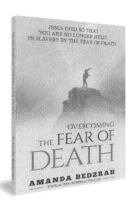

available at

www.amandabedzrah.com

AMANDA BEDZRAH

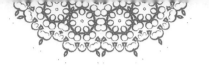

Notes

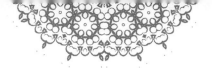

Notes

Notes

....
....
....
....
....
....
....
....
....
....
....
....
....
....
....
....
....
....
....
....
....

Made in the USA
Lexington, KY
15 February 2018